MW00678609

Starts And Stops Along The Way

Sharing Some Stuff
From The Road Most Travel

by
Jim R. Rogers

Pp
PROSEPRESS
www.prosepress.biz

Starts And Stops Along The Way
Copyright © 2012
Jim R. Rogers

Published by Prose Press
75 Red Maple Drive,
Pawleys Island,
South Carolina 29585

proseNcons@live.com
www.Prosepress.biz

Comments: Contact Jim Rogers at
jimrogers@sc.rr.com

ISBN: 978-0-9851889-9-3

Cover/Interior Design: Jim R. Rogers,
        Photo by Sally Z. Hare
 Sea View Inn porch, Pawleys Island, SC

Dedicated to

all of you taking the road most travel

and to

daughter Julie Kay
and her son Daniel
my son Kyle

and to

former wives
Shirley and Kelly

brother Bob
sister Gloria

and especially to

my wife
and inspiration,
my teacher, my friend,
the one who holds my heart
and gives me hope

Sally

special thanks to
Linda Ketron and Larry
Libby Bernardin &
Annie Pott for moving
me forward.

Starts And Stops Along The Way

1.
So This Is It

2.
Seems Like Yesterday

3.
Sit Down And Stay A While

4.
Whose Life Was It Anyway

5.
Ok. Now What

6.
My Time Has Passed

7.
The Road Most Travel

Contents

1.
So This Is It 1

If You're Not Old 2
And Here We Are 3-4
Leave Me Be! 4
Not Yourself 5
Calendar Pages 5
Who Wants To Be Old 6
Starting To Go 6
Not Much Thought 6
Zip Swoosh Zing 7
AARP Is Our Badge 7
Old Man 8
Magic 8
Both 9
How About Reunions 10
Stuff 11
Which Way 11
Talking Along 12
Feeling The Energy 12
Old Glory 13
Your Turn 14-16

2.
Seems Like Yesterday 17

From Birth 18
Out Of The House 19
It Was Supposed To Be 20
Whatever I Have 20

Family 20
When Do You Know 21-22
Decades 22
This I Know For Sure 23
Remember 23
Passion 24
Oldies But Goodies 24
Used To Be 25
Afternoon And Evening Nods 26
Little Things 26
Sides 27
Starts And Stops 28
Your Turn 29-30

3.
Sit Down And Stay A While 31

Visits 32
There Is Pleasure 32
This Is Not Good 33
Love Has Not Been A Stranger 34
Will You Remind Me 35
Spooning 35
Bubble Stuff 36
When You Can Stare 36
Finding Joy 37
Temptations 37
When She Goes 37
Closer 38
Difficult Getting Through 38
PDA 39
Money 39
Grandchildren 40

Son Told Us Today 40
You'll Tell Me 41
We Did Some Things 42
For You 43-44

4.
Whose Life Was It Anyway 45

He Often Envied 46
Think About It 46
Irritations On The Small Stuff 47
OC 47
Two Seniors 48
Feel Like Screaming 48
Even The Most Intimate 48
And Then 49
This Is The Age 49
Sagging 49
Getting Shorter 49
There Is No Bottom 50
When You Get Old 50
TV Is My Challenge 51
It Takes Longer 51
Expand A-Waist 51
Senior Ballet 52
Reinventing Ourselves 52
They Laugh At Us 53
The Older I Get 54
Bothers Me 54
Educate Me? 55
Hair 55
Skin Gets Thin 55
All The $ Went 56

Starts With Squinting 56
For A While 57
It's An Amazing Thing 58
Reading 58
Tired Of Doing It 58
Clothes 59
Can't Talk About It 59
Regimen 60-61
Mom Chose Family Dollar Sweats 62
Growing Apart 63
What We Have Become 63

Extra Blank Pages For You 64-67

5.
Ok. Now What 68

Beliefs 69
Home Work 69
Time 70
Brick By Brick 70
Self Help 71
The Cloudy Day Parts 72-76
Good Morning! 77
When I Started Getting Less Busy 77
Staying So Long 78
Sitting In A Room 79
Who 79
Not Too Concerned 80
Experience Counts For Something 80
Retiree Envy At A Fall Festival 81
Flags Of Our Fathers 82
I'm Not As Good 82

My Hectic Busy Life 83
No News 83
Epiphany On The Roof 84
It's Building 85
Finance 85
Timing 85
Old People Are Problems 85
Dogs 86
Inside Work 87
Can't Do It 87
I Know I'm Right 87
All My Life 88

Ramblings Far From Dementia 89—101

For You 102-103

6.
My Time Has Passed 104

Volunteer 105
Something So Mundane 105
I Cry Over What Should Be 106
I'm Not Dead 106
Still Doing 106
Who Served 107
We Matter 107
They're Gone Under 108
There's A Picture Of Me 108
When We Start Reflecting 109-110
We Are Here To Grow 110
Waiting 111
Criticize 111

When You Have Nothing To Do 111
So Much To Do 112
Gone 112
Paralyzed 113
Took The Less Traveled Path 113
Will 113
Three Things 114
Here's One 114
Anger 114
What I Owe 115
Luck 116
Your Turn 117-118

7.
The Road Most Travel 119

The Only Way 120
Best Friends 121
New Best Friends 121
One 122
We Don't Know It 122
When Her Mother Was Sick 123
Thinking 124
Old Folks Are Slow To Panic 125
Children 125
Ailments Abound 126
Friends No More 126
Getting Harder To Remember 127
Visiting Questions Unanswered 127
All The Time We Hear It 128
She Faded 128
Giving Up Giving In 128
What You Put In 129

Place 129
How We Do It 130
She Settled In To Die 130
Home 131
Don't Take It 132
Dependent 132
Love Life 132
Last Night 133
Don't Care For Me 134
Fear Is A Scary Thing 134
How To Keep Going 135
Clichés 136
Let's Say 137
Closets 138
That's It 139
Your Turn 140-146

Biography 143

1.

So This Is It

If you're not old, stop.
Don't read this
You won't understand it.
Save it 'till you can
Or give it to someone who
Might
Be Old
Then they can give it back to you
When you're old
With input.
Old? Only you know.
For me
Invisible
Even in crowded rooms
Profound! words of wisdom ignored
Less profound
Not even heard
Eyes and ears turned away
Too old to contribute
Or to talk about
Current issues
They think we think how we used to do it
New ideas
I've had none No
I stopped learning and
Did it the way I always did
Oh yeah. Sure.
Some do some don't
Respectful
Almost
Condescending
Accepting
Placating
Welcome
Phony
Here's something you can do
We have a senior on our board.

And here we are
On the way
To being old
Released from
Corporate
Structure
Mandates
Orders
Expectations
Raising children
Raising cane
And all that required stuff of the early years.
What will it mean?
We don't know
We've never been there before
Others have but
That's them
Now it's us
Set free to be
Younger
Healthier
Empty nestier
For now.
Decisions
Still
But new
Rearranging
The deck chairs on the
Titanic
Where to go
Downsize Upsize
Gated
Apartment
Condo
Parent house out back or attached
Retirement community
The village

The dreaded facility with
nurses.
Real old folk
Yearn to stay
Home values down
Once a second floor
Status
Now
A Challenge
Smart
Senior Friendly Home
Comfort is what we want
Something more
Than shelter
Where we can be us
Where we have
Memories.
Where we can
Age in place
Where we can be
Old Folks AT Home

±

Leave me be!
But don't leave me
Alone.

Not Yourself
You're not acting like
yourself
they said.
I've never been who I am before,
so I don't know if I am myself
or not.

The problem is that
you don't know what you want to be when
you grow up until you grow up and then
it's most likely too late to start.

±

Calendar pages.
One by one
They come
And
Go.
They don't mean
Anything at all
Unless we
Want them to
In the mind
In the heart
In the desire
In the joy of
Being alive
To turn
Another page.

Who wants to be
> **Old**
> Not he
> Not she
> Not I
> Not we
> But we are.
> So we
> be.

> ±

> **Starting to go**
> You feel it
> You know.
> Oh no
> Some go soon
> Others wait
> Why is that.
> Learning how to live with
> Loss.
> Learning what we
> Have to.

> ±

Not much thought at the time
about who our children would be.
Not much effort to help them get there.
Here.
Maybe too late to do much now.
Maybe not.

zip. swoosh. zing.
those are the sounds it made as it went by.
It started slow enough, young eyes sparkling
with discovery
finding the joy in it wanting each day to last
longer than the one before especially summer.
And they did drag sometimes, mostly when you
wanted to date, to drive, to smoke, to drink, to
be left alone.
And then you are. How fast it goes now.
Twice the speed of light.
Hard not to fall off.
Not what you thought.
Not what you dreamed.
Not where you wanted to be now
But here you are.
So?
Cares get more refined.
Time is told in different ticks and tocks.
No stones left to un-turn.
Shirts and pants don't match and once I wore
two different shoes
No one noticed.
±

AARP is our badge
to inform, advocate
guide our paths away from ignorance
with dignity, respect
like 91% of us over 65 have at least one
chronic condition (thanks for that)
and sell us really tacky mail order clothes
shoes that don't need lacing.
Sex aids! Because it's never too late And
sticks with springs and claws for reaching
where our bodies won't go.

7

Old Man
When we watched the playback of the
Christmas video it hit me over the head like
a ton of bricks
I was an old man.
While I wasn't looking I had aged
I had not been unhappy really
and I had been healthy
and I had been doing my work well and
supported and loved
so how the hell did I get so old so fast.
I knew it was time for me to actually do
something with my life
fulfill my purpose
make a real difference
do something for god's sake
or one morning I would wake up dead with
the excuse that I had been too busy
or I really didn't know what to do
or how to do it
so I did something else.
±
Magic.
Eating in my Chair
Watching TV
Makeshift pillow as table
Napkins　Towels　Bib
Try hard and
Still spill
Food on my clean
Shirt
Again.

Both

It's hard not being who I was
but now it's so.
I still am some
at least the parts that count
some things don't and it's a good thing
since hair is gone, muscle is less, get up and go is
missing, joints need oil.
age is sneaky
you know it's back there lurking, waiting
all of a sudden, overnight
there it is in the mirror
in others' eyes
it's the disappear potion
and it works as you are no longer seen.
No one takes you seriously
old stories are just that
and they don't count for much
except to you.
Only a few regrets
and only because of sadness
and pain you may have caused
and you have no idea about
what's next
how could you really
how could anybody?
no one has been there to tell it
to share it
so you live each hour
like the last and mull
and try not to hurt again
or end up on the line somewhere
believing that what has been
was a cruel joke or an
extraordinary privilege.
Of course. It's
Both.

How about
Reunions
Went to one
Knew none
Until
Faces came
Through
Wrinkles
Spots
Sag
Time
And there
They were
Classmates
Again
Shining
Smiling
Faking
Appearing
In spite of
It.

Stuff
From years
Stacks and
Layers
From room to room
And paths
And detours
To bed
What to do
Where to go
Who wants
What's there
On the walls
In the halls
Shelves so
Full
Boxes now
What to do
Out they go
Here I stay.
±
Which way
I could have done this or
I could have done that
but not both
how the hell do we choose
we don't
It chooses us.

Talking along
And
Bam
Can't think
Of the next
Word.
Stalled
In mid sentence
While they wait
To see
If I
Make it

±

**Feeling the
Energy**
Draining out
Meds galore
To plug the dike
A tug of war
Science
Vs.
Nature
Who will win
Who do you think.

Old Glory
Smiles, and happy times and much more than a lot
not encumbered.
  They rested there reclined in the folds of my mind
knowing but not knowing that someday they would
stretch and unfurl once again to wave in the winds of
life.
  It feels good to fly, to be exposed to the elements, to
sag one minute, only to burst forth with currents of
emotion not allowed to be for fear of pain, for fear of
another loss, a loss of something never had.

  Notice the edges ... wear, starting to tear, eating into
the very heart of the design across which stitches and
patches have been applied holding it together for yet
another reveille and taps hoping for a longer day to
separate the two and sunshine is best.
                    It only fades the colors.
  Flag bearer, flag bearer feel how soft I am
how thin I am, sometimes.
            You as one so close can almost see clear
through.
                              Saluted.
                         Applauded.
                         Honored.
                         Protected.
                         Pitied.
                         Extended.
            Retired.
Hang it on a flat wall In the den or frame it behind glass.
        No more wind.
    No more sunshine.
  Only pool and sometime parties and pro bowls and
empty tv.
  Occasionally
                    an admiring eye who sees what once
            was there.

YOUR TURN!

I can almost hear you saying,

"I can do this stuff."

And you are right. You can.

So I have included a few blank

pages at the end of each section

offering you some space for your

own thoughts, your own memories

in your own words on your

own aging journey.

Have fun. I did.

WRITE IT DOWN!

Can't believe I'm 60.
A nice round number

They say 60 is the new 40
yet,
I really am slowing
down.

Not in my prime.
Time to shift
to

who knows?

60 is the new 40
but maybe the energy is
internal

maybe my work is to be so
connected to

the dance
of all that is.
How well can I do that
job?

WRITE IT DOWN!

2.

Seems Like Yesterday

From birth
there was sunshine
and happy days
and Twain friends

and caring parents
friendly neighbors
inspiring teachers
and grandstand cheers

The world was small
and simple
complications were
way off somewhere.

Special and
destined to be
somebody different
than they had ever known

Everybody thought it
and he took it
and began the race
that he knew nothing about

Ill prepared
but eager
full of hope
he took his steps.

Tomorrows
became todays
became the past
and what of
life?

18

Out of the house
I went
away from all
that I knew
feeling the world
like never before
eyes wide heart ready
brain growing
each one
fresh
exciting
worrisome
then scary
then too many
one
two
three
more
teachers
giving
getting some
but not enough
one so
odd and
would not fit
one so bright
so right
so wrong
maybe home
was best
no way it's so
just go and go and go.

It was supposed to be simple, clear, direct, and even easy. But it just got complicated.
There was no way a young and idealistic boy
from a Norman Rockwell town could have
prepared for what he got
On the Job training.

Whatever I have
Is what I've got
No more No less
It's mine
I worked hard
Lived long
Loved many
Lost some
Laughed a lot
And cried.
Whatever I have
It's mine
Whatever it is.

±

Family.
Glue
That holds
Us together
Gets
Too hot and
Melts
And the
Pieces
Fall
Apart
But
Stay
Sticky.

When do you know it's time for a change
Where does the idea first come from?

A distant spot of sail on the mind's horizon gliding
slowly toward you getting fuller and bigger and
closer and stronger as it sensitizes your knowing of
the wind
Does it grow like a seed in the ground, getting larger
and healthier as its environment of need waters and
nurtures it to blossom and beautifully lulls you into
the notion that you had better move from where you
are. Sometime soon.
Or maybe it starts as a mental cold sore, causing just
a hint of the pain that is to come unless you do
something
but of course you don't know all that unless you've
gone through such change before and if you have
then why are you letting yourself in for all that shit
again?

 It could be that you are just sick and tired of
being sick and tired as the 12 steppers say.
You could be just stuck in a mud rut, adjusted to the
goo and slow movement and not do anything but stay
stuck.

 Then, there's that classic cliché
when the pain of staying is worse than the pain of
leaving
That's when you have to change
To do otherwise would be totally foolish
And yet being foolish doesn't seem to matter
When I am deep into dysfunctional comfort
I don't care if I'm foolish or not
I care about whether or not I am happy
But, even then happiness is so fleeting
One minute high, another low

I always feel empty when I'm happy…and guilty
It won't last long and there are so many others
who aren't. So, I don't do anything.
They say that's a decision.

It is just too much trouble.
I don't think I can change.
Not if my life depends on it. Maybe it does. Naa.
What's the big deal? I'm just hot that's all
and I need to cool this room down.
Now let's see. Is it up to cool or down to cool?
Never can get that straight.

 Should I take a chance, or wait for somebody who
knows?   I think I'll wait.
For now. Maybe.   ±

Decades
So many
So many
Of us
So many
Paths
We took
So many
Stories To tell
So much
Happened
In our
Decades
So many
Of us
So alike
So different

So what

This I know for sure
Sitting too long in one place
Feeling like the world has passed you by and
Woe is you
Because you're old
Will push
You deeper Into the pluff mud
Of nothing
Into more nothing
Until
You
Disappear
But
Doing something
Any something
Will move you
Activate you
And one grows
Into more then
Many and many gets you going again
Nike has it right.
Just do it.
±

Remember
Long distance calls
How special they were
How we
Planned them
Looked forward to them
Used them sparingly
Amazing
Miracle of the times.
How I miss those
And hand written
Notes of thanks
Of
Hello How Are You.

Passion
Used to
Drive me
Got me up
To go
To do
Got me up
For that too
Knew I could
Energize
When
Needed
Get it done
Make 'em
Applaud
See how good I am
Where has it gone
Away from me
And I can't seem to find it again &
I had nothing to say about it.
±
Oldies but Goodies
We listen to
Music that we
Love
Danced
Closely
Whispered
Stuff
That came to be
Doing it
Still
Loving it
Still
Now that we are
Oldies
Goodies.

Use to be
Just three
And sometimes
Less
Early morning
Daytime
Till midnight
Cheap
Entertainment
On
The tube
Now
Wow
A
Vastland
Of choices
Twenty four hours
Seven days
Three hundred sixty five
Everywhere
You look
Listen
So much
There
Not much
There.

±

Afternoon and Early evening Nods
Come
And I can't
Stop them
Tired
Run down
Bored
Indolent
Snorts wake me
Ashamed
When I don't respond
To a question
React to a bogey
Or participate in conversation
Is this the sleep
Before the Sleep.

±
Little things
You never thought
To be Hard
Are.
Just getting
Out of a
Chair
Without
Soreness
Pain
Grunting
Pushing
Pulling
Regretting
Accepting
Limitations
That come with the
Territory.

Sides
All
Through
The
Vastland
Countless
Commercials
Telling us
Who to be
How to be
When to be
What to be
And the
Medications
The best of all
Helping
Anew
But
Watch out
For
The sides

Nausea
Headaches
Bloat
Weight loss or
gain
Hives
HBP
LBP
Gout
Diarrhea
Constipation
Depression
Anxiety
Mood swings
Lost wages
Shortness
Tallness
Death
Mother in law
blues
Mass Murder
tendencies
Rose hater
Terrorism Tactics
And so on
Unbelievable
Not me
Sticking with
What I've got.

Along the way
Many starts
Many stops
Checking in to see
What was there for me
Found and lost
Lost and found
People
Places
Things
Feelings
Ideas
Beliefs
Hopes
Dreams
Realities

Starts and stops along the way.

YOUR TURN. Space for you.

FOR YOU.

3.

Sit Down And Stay A While

Visits
One, two
Three, four
Five, six
The monthly
Visits now
Agreed places
Where we go
Together
Hand
In
Hand
But not in step
Thank god.

±

There is
Pleasure in having
Been here
This Long
Just lucky I guess
Gave
Took
Lived
Worked
Played
Loved and
Found some, too.

32

This is not good

You have captured my body. Yet
You have freed it to feel fine tuned, honed
For you and you alone, always ready for
Your touch. Hungry still after for even more.

    This is not good.
Not only have you captured my body
You have captured my time.
It's all yours. I try to give it somewhere else.
I even do it.
But it's not without you standing close, smiling.

    This is not good.
Not only have you captured my time
You have captured my mind.
It knows the countless things it must attend.
There and energized yes.
But never as a single. You always sing duet.
 I even try to push you out, but when the touch
A grasp instead.

    This is not good.
You have not only captured my body my time
my mind
You have also captured my soul.
Your light is warm and peaceful. Your glow
Turns my gray and used and tired to renewed hope
Overflowing joy. Belief in so much more.
Colors now and useful once again.

    This is not good.

This is a miracle.

Love has not been a stranger to me
I have known her.

She embraced my mother and me
And my father in an entirely different way.
She showed me her way with my brothers and
cousins and aunts and grandmother and friends
although looking back that may have been
something else.

As I grew, she showed me more and let me love
A wife in a way that I could then. There was care
And caring but there was always still me.
Later, she introduced me to passion and that was
good.
And then came romance and then came otherness.
Out of nowhere love matched me to another who
knew her in a different way but a way that made me
feel Loved.
 I finally arrived at the ultimate love, I thought.
She gave two a connection and a bond and that, too,
was good.
And then she changed course. Love was redefined.
It became something else. Romance waned. Passion
cooled. Only care remained. And otherness.
Confused and despondent. How could it have become
something else?
And now I know. It changed to become.
Love has gently warmed her way deep into a place I
didn't know existed. She has revealed a part of her
that goes way beyond anything imagined.
She has let me have this time with her very own
incarnation.
She has given me her self.

She has given me you.

Will you remind me to tell them to
fix the overhead light in the car?
Who's going to remind me?
Let's leave notes.
Remember to do that.
You remember to do that.
Ok. Ok.

I forgot.
You remembered.
You forgot
I remembered.
Takes two of us to make a good one.
±

Spooning
The greatest pleasures
And comforts of the day
Any day
Are those when the last light is out
The dogs are quiet
The nite lights are soft
And I snuggle up
And hold you gently firm
Being just where I want to be
then
It's your turn to hold me
Even better.
We fit.

Bubble Stuff
 She called him her "bubble stuff".
He had mixed emotions about it
When they were alone he blushed a bit
Smiled and he wanted to rub up against
her cat like
and get whatever else she had.
When she used it in mixed company
even with close family he would give
her a look that said "that's private"
flush red and retreat to another
room of conversation
or busy himself in the kitchen
His daughter thought it was cute
and sweet.
She liked that finally
someone adored her dad.
±

When you can stare
at your wife in bed beside you
mouth open
snoring a bit
and you can smile with warmth in your
heart and say to yourself
she's so cute when she does that.
When you can gently smooch the
wrinkles under her chin
brush her crows feet and
mouth lines with your lips and
flash a genuine smile with a
of course I love you
you do.

Finding joy
Was a daily discovery in youth
Except for the disappointments
That came, the hurt, the heartbreaks.
Made me strong and wise
So today I can still have joy
With the disappointments,
The hurt, the heartbreaks.
±

Temptations
Galore.
Sitting there
Staring
Just asking us to take
Eat, drink, buy, speak, risk, try, go, stay, feel, give,
keep.
Ignore
Sure
Easy
Not
Use wisdom
Ha
Use will
Ha. Ha.
±

When she goes
I go too. But I stay
Moping in aloneness
Missing Sighing Pitying
My self
Awful sandwiches with calories and fat
And absence of a heart that likes to listen
Looking for her return to
Her place with me.
She does.
This time.

Closer please
I can't get any closer
Try
She did
And did.

±
Difficult
Getting through
The days
Feeling like no purpose
Tired of
Doing stuff
I don't really want
To do
Tired of going
Just to be going
Tired
Just tired.
Then you come
I smile and
Want you
Filled with energy
Forgetting tired
It comes from another place.

PDA
Public display of affection
PDA
Private display of affection
Either is fine with me
For some
Emotion
Varies
Shy
Shame
Proud
Private
Cute
Sweet
Well
A little hand-holding never hurt anybody
PDA
Private
Well now
That's
Another
Matter
Ours.   ±

Money
Not a problem now
Things
Got plenty now
Time
Very little now
All the same
Now
We are.

Grandchildren
Come and go
Like children
Leaving us behind.
Their life
Their choice
Like we did.

But before taking off
What pride
What angst
What pain
What worry
What joy
What memories.

± **Son**
Told us today
That he and
Family would
Not join us
For this holiday
They see us
All the time
So they
Are going
Somewhere
Else to see
Someone Else
They
Don't see
So often
We understand
Completely
Hello
New
Rationed
Parents

You'll tell me

If I have food in my beard
If you'll tell me I have spinach on
my tooth
If I talk too loud
If I talk too much
If I repeat myself
If my jokes aren't funny
If the blackheads show
If the hairs need tweezers
If I eat too fast
If I'm unkind
If I'm fading fast
If I'm still pretty
If I'm still a hunk
Oh, yes. Still.
OK then.
We're fine.

We did some things.

A place where smiles come easy
The couch is a teddy bear for many.

Finding comfort even in discord
The place is safe enough for honest
words.

The time together renews the bond
The people there embrace the you.

There was a hole now pushed way back
Filled in with growth that time can give.

Gifts and food and care abound
That place we nurture and get it from.

How they long to greet the roots
We made it strong and holds us well.

 Home.

FOR YOU.

FOR YOU.

4.

Whose Life Was It Anyway

He often envied those who knew why they had been born.

The natural athlete, or explorers or teachers who never even thought about being anything else. They came to do a certain job, and they did it, got very good at it and were honored for having given their all to a job or to others.

He could have gone in so many different directions. He had some talent in many areas...and choosing one or even two proved to be melancholy now in his last years.

He often wondered if he had gone in another direction, what would his life had been like. If he had chosen to pursue his first love, or even his second, would it have made any difference in how he felt now?

±

Thoughts about it all
Maybe tell her
Now that he has been dead for a year
Cancer got him young
Thought about it all
And how dying early
Takes care of any
Old age
Second guessing
And wondering
About what comes next
And whether we did
All we wanted to or
We bog down in
Misery of Lost Life
And regrets. No
Don't
Tell
Her
She knows.

Irritations on small stuff
Come more often and quicker
Impatience with an open drawer
Those ads inserted in magazines
That have to be ripped out
Stickers on my apples
And remains of stickers on my gifts
How thin can they make paper
Wasting time trying to turn a page
The dirty dish in the sink
Stacks of stuff in the way
The way she says no now
The way she never says yes
The way he rolls his eyes
The way we turn our backs in bed
In life.
±
OC
Obsessive Compulsive at 75.
Really.
Just another detail that
Pisses me off
The cleaning lady didn't
Put it back like it was.
A cleaning lady?
This is where
That belongs
Somebody hung my robe on the wrong peg
The towel is not in
The right place
And there's
A place for everything
And everything
In its place
Like me.

Two seniors
Giving each other
The middle finger
In the parking lot
At the post office
Both right.
Both wrong.
Does it really matter.
Seems to
To them.
±

Feel like screaming
Unfair
Unjust
Rude
Ignorant
Incompetent
Intolerant
Inconsiderate   ±
Mean   **Even**
Hands tied   **The**
Mouth shut   **Most**
Inside heat   **Intimate**
With no where to go.   **Friends**
                       Never
                       Know
                       About
                       The
                       Sagging
                       Balls
                       In
                       The
                       Toilet bowl
                       Water.

And then
First with the prostate
Sitting to pee
Standing
Took too long to finish.
Multi stops on trips
Movies not over two hours
Biopsies
Benign
Lucky
But roto rooter
Still sitting
Now challenged by
All low commodes with
High water
±
This is the age
Where men make
Close friends of
urinals
±
Sagging
Comes
Slowly
Oozing forth
Changing waists
Hell NO to T- shirts
Avoiding mirrors
Attention
±
Getting
Shorter was
A surprise.
Another
Unexpected
Gift
Of Aging.

There is
No
Bottom
To the
Depth
Of
Pain
We feel
When
There is
Loss
Moms
Dads
Brothers
Sisters
Friends
But the worst
By far
The deepest
Pain
Loss of
Your
Child.

±

When you get old
Your body starts making noise
Starts talking to you
Snap crackle and pop joints
With vocal accompaniment
Groans, moans, ows and ohs and a few
dammits.
Hurts to move
To roll over   To readjust.
It hurts to change positions
and opinions.

TV is my challenge.
So much wrong and
I catch them at it
Yelling at the stupidity
Of officials
Of commercials
Politicians
City officials
City officials
Celebrities
Politicians
You think that's good!
I think it stinks!
No one cares.
I do.
±

It takes longer to tie the shoes
Finding new ways
Bending Lifting
Sitting
On the floor In a chair On a stool
Crooking the leg
Asking for help
Velcro
Slippers
Barefoot
±

Expand-a-waist pants
Genius
Fit like a glove
Pride lost to bulge
Why not shirts
Now go
To Goodwill after 20 years
Button strain
Larger size
Breath holding time reduced 20%

Senior ballet
One legged
Dancing
Not holding on
Putting foot
In pants
Under wear
Panty hose
Finding balance
Being graceful
And fearful
That it will
Get worse.

±

Reinventing
Ourselves
Is what
We're
Supposed to do
But
I like me as I am.

They laugh at us.
I know. I used to.
We wear strange clothes
They're old
Why get new
They think we have bad taste.
They don't know that we just
Don't give a shit.
We don't deserve it all
Not all.
But some for sure
Loud
Self centered
Selfish
Demanding
Don't listen
Talk
A lot
About
Our lives
Where we came from
What we did
Who we were
When we were.

The older I get, the more pissed off I get.
It's no wonder old people get cranky with age
      they see the end
      they didn't get it all done
      they didn't do anything they wanted to do
        much less everything they wanted to do
No time to start over.
Trying to contribute
Get $\pm$
disrespect
demeaned   **Bothers me**
discouraged   People who
Pissed off   park
Like never before.   in no parking
                             handicapped
                             wrong lane
                             wrong way
                             take up two
                             parking spaces
                             biggest suv
                             on the block
                             people in
                             movies
                             talking loud
                             at wrong times
                             leave during
                             credits blocking
                             view of others
                             Rudeness
                             Inconsiderate
                             Hard to tolerate
                             rudeness
                             It's all about
                             that
                             For me
                             Pissed off.
                             Again.

Educate me?
I don't want to know
All that stuff
That will make me
Happier
Healthier
Richer
Wiser
Skinnier
Smarter
Social
I just want to be
Me.

±

Hair growing where
It shouldn't
Not growing where
It should.

You know

Hair today
Gone tomorrow.

±

     Skin gets thin
     Letting through those
     Dark places
     The red, black, blue
     Road maps
     That were hiding there
     All along.

All the $ went
To someone
Not me
And now I sit wishing regretting wondering
Mad as hell
Sad too
And not knowing
What's next
Plans I had derailed
Accidents
Fate
Illness
Injury
Things happen
Unintentional detours along the way
Plans changed
There's no turning back.
Can rewind
And look at it
Pause and reflect on it
But it's done
Can't change what was.
Can change what might be.
±

Starts with squinting
Looking for light
Stretching arms
Holding too close
Ends with glasses
Bi   Tri
Thick
Thank god for
Big letters.

For a while
I bitch
I moan
I complain
until I see a young man
in a wheelchair
driving it with his chin
and then I realize how lucky I am
   for a while
I whine
I lament
I yell unfair

until I see a man with cerebral palsy painfully
inching his way down the sidewalk
greeting people with an awkward smile
and then I realize how lucky I am
   for a while
I get depressed
I become desperate
I panic

until I see a homeless woman shivering
among her cart full of worldly possessions in a dark
alley
and then I realize how lucky I am
   for a while
I see frail
I see fear
I see no hope

what does it take to be
permanently grateful.
being a homeless, wheel-chair
moving victim of cerebral palsy
And becoming frail, fearful and hopeless?
   I hope not.

It's an amazing thing
Chest
Settles into groin and hips
Hiding what was once
Seen and touched
Need still there
Motivation for access
Resignation to the loss
Choices.

±

±

Reading
TV
Hers
His
Sometimes
His
Hers
Mostly
Each other's
Home life
It works.

Tired of doing it
Not that
We still do that
Some don't believe it.
Tired of
Pinching pennies
Writing monthly checks
Waiting for a real person on
the phone
Waiting for the kids to call
A thank you note
Brushing teeth
Combing my hair
Taking pills
Doctor's appointments
Procedures
Required social time
Bridge
Walking at the mall
Shopping
Golf
Drinking
Not remembering
What's good.

Clothes
Comfort not style
Except to
Impress the others at the
Dragged-to
Socials
Meetings
Worships
Weddings
Funerals
A lot.
So few
Look
Fewer
Care.   ±

Can't talk about
Hemorrhoids
Gout
Gas
Pimples
Flatulence
Psoriasis
Operations
Procedures
Children
Politics
Religion
Savings
Stock market
Neighbors
In laws
But
We do.

Regimen
Struggle up
Pee
Robe
Hands, Face, hair
Hand cream
Age defying! Love that one.
Glasses
Where are they
Slippers
Kitchen
Coffee
Water
Newspaper outside
TV
Banana
Health bar
Peanut butter on
something
Pills, wake up,
not too much,
gerd, heart, strength,
vitality, bones, aches,
multi-vision
whatever's left
Coffee
TV
Bathroom

Then

Newspaper
TV
Coffee
Walk
Aquacize Flirt Shower
Office
Calendar
Nothing
Computer
Nothing
Email
Nothing
TV Nothing
Lunch Cereal
Sunday Times
Magazines
Meetings maybe
Walk the dogs
Organize
Reminisce
TV
Plan tomorrow. Tough.
Drinks Dinner
TV Book
Pre bed
Similar
Post bed
Late TV
Some sleep
Start again
Ahhh
The Good life.

Mom chose Family Dollar Sweats

Gave her Belk's blouses
That stayed in the boxes
Still the sweats
Why
Mom
Easier
Finding
Choosing
Maintaining
Cold wash
No iron
Three colors
Black, grey, and navy blue
Soft
Comfy
We were frustrated
Bewildered
Now know
How smart she was
Now it's us
Just
Nicer sweats
More Colors

Growing apart
It's called now
Growing together
It should be
Could be.
±
What have we become
Where is what we were
Along the way
The disconnect
That
We vowed
Would not be us
And here we are
Together but
Apart
Wondering
Grieving what was
Hoping
For
Something else
Something
That was

Again

Kind of scary thinking about
physical challenges + infirmities,
as well as greater irritibility,
7 people c life r depends
distance from Ward that my
happen. At the same time, I'm
writing about + deeply appreciative
for the small aspects of
mundane, daily living.

FOR YOU.

FOR YOU.

FOR YOU.

5.

Ok. Now What

Beliefs
Practicing what
We preach
Or not.
So many ways
From so many places
BaskinRobbins flavors
It works
Most of the time
Some think everybody else
Is wrong
Same goals
Heaven
Not hell
Will we get where
Up to each.

±

Home work
In youth
Chores, self, clothes, room, bed, trash
School
Home work
More school
Home work
Job
Home work
Life
Home work
Living, teaching, growing, failing, falling, moving on
Our own Home
More Work
Home work
Still.

Time
it's been going on for some time now
and I think I have learned some things

Here's one

I don't waste as much time as I used to
The process of getting to depression
and coming out again is shorter

I can go to the suicide mode
and up to euphoria almost immediately
without messing around
with all that stuff in between.
±

Brick
By
Brick
I build my Wall
Ten feet wide
And
Twice as tall
Yes I wonder
When
They say
That Wall
Is it protecting you
Or
Is it
In your way.

self help

book shelves lined with volumes
soul searching philosophy
simple and deeper poetry
for sale psychology
from infomercials.

a lot has helped a little
a little has helped a lot
a storehouse of searching
a library of life

along with others
I've needed all the help
I could get
to face the unexpected firing squad.

in it all I made a find

the best single aid for
grief, loss, depression,
frustration, confusion,
rejection, desperation,
anger, hurt, loneliness
and all of the more
is to
have a little money in the bank.

The cloudy day parts.
A summary of the whole.

why tell anyone about the shit?
it lets you know i'm human. it lets me know i'm
not alone. it helps me get rid of it.
*

i sit here in the California spring, but it's winter
in my heart. my mind tells me it's a place i'm in
that's all. it will go away tomorrow. it's
happened before. this time, i'm not sure. it feels
like it might stay for a while. or longer. until i
make it go away. this time, i'm scared.
*

when i first came i was hugged a lot. mother,
mammie, cousins. it made me feel special and
loved. it gave me some self worth sense. i had
enough in storage to last a long time. until
yesterday.
*

now it comes to this. realities obscure the
dreams. what plans i had! it all seemed right. i
thought i had a purpose. i was actually going to
do something wonderful and memorable.
*

and now? i've left a trail of sadness, frustration,
heartbreak, and regret behind my egocentric
self. i thought i was helping. i thought i was
giving. i thought i was planting seeds for
growth.
*

my ladies are alone and sad. i wasn't smart
enough to make it. my children are confused.
they look to me and i have no truths to tell them.
i can not give them guidance. i am lost myself.
*

things came. the winds blew and i went with
them. i've never been able to start the breeze
and follow it through the trees.
*

the first faint colors of my own mortality have
begun to glow around the outer defenses of my
living. barely visible now, i know they are there.
and they will get brighter and closer. mostly
they are shades of foreboding gray. sometimes
and getting more often, they are pastel and
pleasing and inviting.
*

i don't plan well. so many times i've built a road
and on it traveled for a while. each time, there
were pot holes, mud puddles, and side exits that
took me off into a thicket of nothing. returning, i
would proclaim in pain that the journey was
much too rough. and then i'd build a new road.
and start out again. looking.
*

i've finally found what lonely is. listening again
and again to a missed phone call message on my
answering machine.
*

where have all my friends gone? where i sent
them with my isolation and self absorption.
perhaps i asked them to be someone else.
perhaps i don't give enough.
*

i have seen talent.
i have seen vision.
i have seen brilliance.
i have seen genius.
i have seen greatness.
 but of these, i am none.
what, then, am i?

i have seen
and i know
what i am and what i am not.
i am just...i am.
*

i keep listening for that voice
to tell me what to do.
that voice i keep listening for i know now
of course is mine.
*

when you live out of cardboard boxes
you live a cardboard life.
*

i arrived at the party too late. the main course
was already being served and i could not get the
host's attention. i never liked parties anyway.
*

my mind seems to stall
in the middle of nothing.
*

i've stopped by
the side of this
road way too
long.
there is very little
chance that today
i am what i was,
or that what i
was, i am today.
perhaps it
means
i am not yet what i was to be, or i was
what i have to re-be.
somewhere
i am sure there is me.
*

limbo. it's not a good place. waiting for
something to happen. for someone to decide.
about things that will affect my life. i could
just say to hell with them. but i can't do that.

there's too much at stake. so. i wait. and the
waiting makes me age. i lose hair.
i get wrinkles. my skin sags. but i wait.
how much longer?
*

yes, i look. my head a spinning top. i ache to
find eyes looking into mine. some glimmer
of encouragement. an invite to enter in.
to open up.
*

approval. accomplishment. affirmation. it's
been so very long since i've had any.
i used to get it have it all the time.
and it went away.
i must be doing something wrong.
no one says i like you. my atta boys have
disappeared. on the job. in the home. in the bed.
i don't get calls to help. i get calls for help.
mostly from myself. and i can't.
*

it scares me most of all. it used to never even
enter my mind. i went so long without it and
now it hounds me. i'm afraid of even more.
rejection. no one's applauded me in such a long
time. how am i supposed to live without it.
*

there is this strong feeling that i need someone
in my life. i don't like it.
there
is
no
one
in my life
i don't like it
l'm not stupid. i know l have choices.
the barb is how to choose from the
choices. do i choose for me?
it seems that that's what i've done. but
i didn't think so.
and that didn't work. be more selfish?
or less?
i don't know.

*

connected. connected to the past. to people.
to places. to ways of doing things. there is
a sense of honor. of duty. holding on to
what i know i knew. dare l break the cord that
keeps me there? dare i take the risk.
dare i not.
*

cloudy days are cold. the light is covered
and i can't see. but, i know it's there.
i have to punch holes, or light a fire. or
simply turn on a switch. i have to do something.
i can only feel good about myself if
i am doing something to feel good about.
i am the only one who cares about me.
only i can change that.
the first thing i'm going to do is
change the way i write I.
*

have I used up the source? it was given
to me and it's kept we me sane. not focused.
but sane. I have to tap into the
place it was and dig even deeper.
I can't be gone, because I am still here.
I am alive. I am well. I am me and
I do want me to be.
*

To begin again. Climb out of the
bowels of depression. I see sun rays
seeping through my closed blinds.
It's out there waiting to make me warm
once more. I Just have to go out there and get
in it. I'll make more mistakes, and I'll develop
more regrets but
I'm not going to die today.

Good Morning!
I love the way a new day feels.
Those few moments when
Yesterday's memories
Are slept into a docile file for later.
When rest gives birth to new eyes
That see a life with energy and hope
And a chance to try again.

±

**When I started getting less
busy**, I became less focused and
driven.
I didn't know how to handle non
hectic to-do time, and I would
forget stuff, 'cause I wasn't
pressured to remember.
I would put off stuff, what's the
big deal...like the one I hate
most, paying by due dates.
Then getting
angry when they charge
the late fee.
I still do it.
All the time.
I'm in charge here.

Staying
So long
Keeps so much
Stuck in Place
Pictures
On walls
Nick and nacks
On tables
Shelves
Crowding
Closets full
Of never worn
Favorites
No room for more
Stuff
Accumulates
Over
Time
Even the floors
The doors
Show wear
But
A
Slight
Movement
Brings
Discomfort
Dogs bark
Even the
Dust feels
At
Home.

**Sitting
In a room**
Crowded with
Interested
Guests
Hanging on
To the
Speaker's
Words of wisdom
Except
Me
Hard
To
Hear
From where I am
6th row
Ashamed to
Cup my hand
Over
My ear
Both
Sure signs
Of
Age
And
Vanity.

Who
Inspires us.
We do.

Not too concerned about our
appearance. Some anyway.
We wear old clothes...worrying about not
spending that money we may need for
older age, and not to burden
the children and spouses.
We have nothing to gain by looking great
no wo/man's hand to win,
no job to compete for,
no seeking approval from others
cause they don't see us anyway
and the young folks say
look at that old fart/ess
with stripes and checks and pants too
short and tights not right and no style
dress and hair a mess.
And we smile.

±

Experience counts for something
For a while
Then it doesn't matter.
Wrong experience
Not new
No E experience
Not up to date
Too slow
Too deliberate
Too much trouble.
Still
Experience counts for something
It's ours.

Retiree Envy at the Fall Festival

night bugs in a stream of light
like snow flakes caught in a whirlwind
just above the handicapped jiffy johnny
drawn by whatever draws them to such

inside the circus-like tent without stripes
other creatures gathered for the stuff that
draws them to such music mostly from a
mixed group of instruments all not
trained to
perfection but good enough

old and younger, rich and not so much
joined in appreciation of Barber and
Copeland and a short caring conductor
with pianist guest delivered rhapsodies in
blue for multi colored tables decorated
for prizes to come

food and wine and other hidden spirits
aplenty mostly smiles of enjoyment and
standing applause some not fully present
from too much or not enough

and one small boy who out of place stayed
quiet and still as in the dark his focused
face was softly lit by something small
beneath the table's edge.

His something.

Flags of Our Fathers
opened this week.
I went on a rainy afternoon
and it took my breath away.
I didn't cry only because I stopped myself.
And, as almost always
I was the last to leave the theater.
I even stayed longer than usual as the lights
eased on and the ushers flowed into the aisles
wielding their brooms and pans as they pulled
the trash barrels behind them attacking the mess
that was just made mostly by senior citizens who
had just seen Clint Eastwood's version of
another mess made by roughly the same
generation.

Generations often leave messes
for the next ones to clean up.

It must be the law, the order of things or
something.
±
I'm not as good as I thought I was...not as
smart not as special.
I don't know what happened.
Hard to admit
We don't know it all
Mother had drawers
Too stuffed to open
Why, mom?
Not smart
Doesn't even make sense.
Now
You should see my drawers
If I could open them.

My hectic
Busy life is slowing down now
My plan
As I have the time to think
Often actually clearly
Is to think clearly
I am learning that there are many more people than I
Who are more special than I
Or who have probably suffered the same haunting
Thoughts as I
That they too were special and had a special
Contribution to make in their lives
And wonder if it's
Too late.

$\pm$

No news
Is good news
Better than
What we see
Hear
Day after
Day after
Day
Printed
Television
Radio
Painting pictures of
How bad
It is
How bad it's going
to Be
And no
Slowing down
So
No more news for
me
I'll make my own
Thank you.

Epiphany on the roof
Due to age
had to change the way I do things
no longer strength, athleticism, balance
now has to be planning,
not taking risks,
taking breaks (endurance)
using my brain and staying focused
like not stepping on the electrical cord and
watching my feet slip out from under me and
rolling me off the roof's edge smashing to the
ground in one large grunt with something
broken that will send me to the emergency
room and her into a dither.

While I was creating this new approach to
living longer and taking great pride in my
discovery and losing my focus on the task I
stepped on the electrical cord.
Nope. I did not slip down
This time.
I allowed myself a couple of well phrased
ouch words loud enough for the preacher next
door to hear who responded to my
Jesus Christ! with Praise God!
and I heard her coming.
So much for that.

It's building.
The complexity of it all overwhelms
me and paralyzes my brain.
A global community and so flat
we can see it all at one time
too much to take in
it freezes me in place.

±

Finance
Religion
Retail
Public service
Utilities
Law
Manufacturing
That was us then
Who now?
±

Timing
Reflexes
Waning
Surprising
Reaching for
My wine glass and
Missing
Oops.

±

Old people are
Problems
We hear that
Of course we are
One of our
Entitlements
Should we be
We can be more the
Solution.
Nobody thinks to
Ask.
Don't wait
Tell them
Speak up
Risk it.
What
Do we have
To lose.

Dogs
Einstein and Eleanor Roosevelt
Not kidding
On the daily walk
As long as the journey is
underway
High spirits and jaunty
But when they sense that we are
About to end it and return home
Spirits fall and a meandering
delay
Sets in
As soon as we sense the journey
Beginning to end
We slip into depression and
despair
Rather than enjoying to the
fullest
The time on the trip we have left
and
One more sniff of what's there.

Inside work
Outside work
Those parts of us
Connected for
Life
Who knew
There's
Still time.

±

Can't do it
Can't stop
Can't try
Can't go
Get angry
No
Get
Really angry
Mad
Pissed off!
That might help
Who

±

I know I'm Right!
How could this be wrong?
Why can't Everybody Be Like Me?
Why can't everybody be just like me?
Mr. Perfect.
Then we wouldn't have any problems.
She is smiling.

All my life
there was this feeling way down deep
inside me that I was special.
      All my life
I felt that there was something unique I
was supposed to do.
      All my life
I found myself out of step pretty much
most of the time.
      All my life
I kept looking and listening for the
guidance, the direction, the way.
      All my life
I wondered how it would happen, when it
would happen and how I would handle it.
      All my life
it seemed to be around the next corner.
Hold on a little while longer and you'll
find it.
      All my life
the place I thought I was to be wasn't the
place for long enough to be the final
place.
Here's where I made my mistake
I actually believed what I was told
That what I ended up choosing to be
mattered.
As we age we find that with rare
exceptions
the rank and file common man has little
to do with what happens in the world.
At all.

rambling thoughts
far from dementia

There are days I feel like
I am waking up after a long sleep.
Now that I am slowing down my brain activity
and my physical to-do list, there is more time for
me to see things I haven't noticed in a long time,
or never did, or thought they were too menial to
dwell on at the time. I find myself seeing people,
places, and things...behaviors for the first time.

Things I know
we all have feelings of wanting recognition,
approval,
applause
adults and children alike need involvement,
engagement, inclusion, interest, care
and if we don't get it we become
sad, disappointed, resentful, angry,
uncooperative, and we act out in many ways.

Ranting...I've tried that. Done it a lot. It
always seems to end with no results but
rather regrets over embarrassing those
around me and myself. I want so hard to
be Atticus Finch. I want to be
emotionally mature, conversationally
brilliant, effective in my convictions and
persuasion efforts.

I think I missed that boat.

Our sweetest most loyal dog,
Einstein
in his last days
courage and desire to stay living
because he loved and was loved so
completely.

And Cinnamon had the patience we should all
have. Waiting for hours for just one toss of
the ball
So she could gather her energy, embrace her
life, race to win, bring it back, and wait again.
She found that purpose.

I used to laugh under my breath at the way
some old folks dressed. The leisure suits, the
matching nylon sweat suits with the required
stripe, or the twin tee shirts with "I'm with
stupid" printed on the fronts, the Velcro strap
shoes, the awful taste in the matching of
clothes, stripes with checks, yellows with
greens, greens with blues, (my mother would
croak) those dumb Henry Fonda On Golden
Pond hats, and the list is endless.
I used to think it was because they had no
money as well as no taste. They lived on a
fixed income and couldn't afford nice new
clothes and someone to advise them on what
to choose to wear.

Now that I am one of them, it's not money.
I think I actually remember writing this
earlier, We just don't give a shit.
Some of us, that is.
We aren't trying to win another's heart,
approval, blessing, promotions, or anything.
Why should we care?
Nobody sees us anyway.
And if we really wanted them to,
then wearing this stuff is the surest way
to get their attention.
What was it they used to tell us as young
parents?
Children need attention. If they don't get any,
they will do something to get it. They would
rather have negative attention than no
attention at all.
It must be true.

This is what happens to us old folks
as we realize that we are going to
die.
Not sooner or later, but
sooner than later.
We see it beginning to lift its head
yonder on the horizon and it scares
the hell out of some of us.
We're not ready to go yet.
We still have some fish to fry.

We want to see the grands grow up
and prove that generations do
improve
with each cycle.
We want to see if there is something
we can do to change it all and
make it better.
Not only our lives past, but the lives
of the future old people who as
young folks now
have no idea what's ahead of them.
Hell, neither do I.

Because we have less and less say so, or any
power, or any sense of accomplishment or
achievement…we do a whole lot of
criticizing. Gives us artificial power, a
manufactured coping skill to deal with failure
or a sense of it at least or makes us feel that
we know better. For a while there, as I
unconsciously began to feel the pull of time
gone and not complete, I started to criticize
everything…I mean everything. Well, not
her, even though she did do some stuff that
drove me crazy, but with her, I bit the bullet.
I didn't want to sound like a cantankerous old
curmudgeon.

I criticized the hiway construction, a
natural target. I didn't think they knew
what they were doing. Why did they do
this this way instead of that?
Just didn't make sense.
The on and off ramps were
stupid and the way the SCDOT patched
the roads was a joke. And the town crews,
forget about it!

I even criticized the new football stadium
they were building at our university. It
went up impressively but I just knew that
they hadn't measured right. The playing
field didn't look like it was 100 yards.
It couldn't be.
I actually laughed at myself for that.
That's when I knew I was getting
better...healthier...more hopeful, and that
was due to unloading the "to do" plate
and finding center and clarity.

Last night we watched a video on the life
and work and eventual success of Anne
Lamott. She was a heavy drinker for
years and years and when she finally
stopped, she said she saw life completely
different. It slowed, it became clear and
she not only listened but heard and could
focus on what was meaningful and
important
maybe for the first time.

I feel that way now, but it was the slowing down and revisiting the priority list and wondering what to do with the rest of my few years that changed me. It could have been too much scotch, too, but I don't think so. I never was a drunk...just a regular drinker by habit until my speech slurred a bit and I heard myself.

I did do a lot of wrestling with moral, or ethical, or legal decisions. There have been times when I felt I should speak up and say something to someone about what they were or were not doing.

When I lived in Los Angeles, I actually got activated. I used to tell people that they should not park in a no parking space. Or a handicapped space when they were obviously not. Who were they to do it when others were abiding by the law and being considerate? Most of the time, they told me it was none of my business and to get lost or just go fuck myself. I thought it was my business.

I still do, but if I took action every time I felt it to be in order, I'd spend the rest of my life doing that stuff.

I actually got out of my car once and started directing like a traffic cop, which I learned when I directed a real one in a commercial, I un-jammed a parking lot traffic jam.

When I lived in New York, I actually chastised a store clerk for being rude and uncooperative. To another customer, not me.

I got an unusual sense of well being, warm satisfaction as I pulled the spurs out of his tiny foot one by one. I was for the first time in a long time, totally focused on the task. I stopped, bent down, held onto our new dog Eleanor Roosevelt with the leash around the wrist of my left hand and surgically, I thought, nurtured the pitiful one back to his walking and sniffing.

In those rare times past when I would walk the dogs alone, I would always be in a hurry...I would be walking them on my schedule, at my pace, pulling them and jerking them away from those seemingly endless scents of whatever attracted them and slowed us down. I did to the pups what I did to my children and what I now warn parents about as they try to build some kind of positive relationship with their mysterious offspring while practicing parenting-on-the-run.

It was my normal state of urgency. I have lived most of my life with a to-do list and I was damned good at getting stuff done. I was raised to believe that you are your work and your achievements are the shining stars of success in our world. I had a work ethic so big I almost choked on it. One of many positives handed down to me by my Dad. Character. That was his big thing. He was the most honest man I ever knew. He worked hard his entire adult life, finally living a few years with his camellias and azaleas before cancer got him at 61. I can't cheat. I can't lie. Well, I can't out and out lie. Whites and omissions, yeah, but they don't count in today's world. They counted to my dad, though.

I gave a workshop once and nobody
came. Not even the person who
asked me to do it. I laughed.
It was all I could do.

Some of My Movie Gems
The Hours.
Someone has to die in order for the rest of us
to value life.
My life has been stolen from me.
I thought it was the beginning of happiness.

You cannot find peace by avoiding life.

Lord of the Rings. All you have to do now is
to decide what to do with the time
you have been given...

My favorite movie
Atticus Finch tells his son
There's a lot of bad stuff in the world.
I can't protect you from it all
Following the guilty sentence of Tom
In To Kill A Mockingbird

I feel guilty just sitting on the couch and working hard not to have such a full plate. I feel that I have been given some unique talents...at times I even considered myself a renaissance man, but I believe you have to be really outstanding at at least one thing and pretty good at a lot of others to qualify for that label.
Maybe next time.

People tell me to stop feeling guilty. They tell me to relax and enjoy my last years to the fullest. I have worked and worked hard for over 50 years, which doesn't seem like a lot relatively speaking, but with our life expectancy now about 76 (and 12 of those getting out of high school, another 4 in college, another 3 in the army) you would think that all of those years I worked as did any red blooded American boy would have been enough.
So now I should just quit.

Sure.

Clint Eastwood is doing his best work in his 70s

It's interesting what happens to us as we find ourselves with more time.

Today, I didn't feel stress and pressures of taking care of the to-do list items, since there are few left on the list these days.
So a lot of them fell
Through the cracks. And next month
They will bite me
In the ass.

At what point do I stop saying
gee whiz, golly, oh my, I'm sorry if I
caused you to misbehave...that you
approach life differently than I...like
those cutting people off in traffic, no
signal, jumping in line
insurance companies not paying for
procedures
Medicare mess,
rude and incompetent clerks
politicians who don't get it
no follow up on calls, or activity.
no return calls.
consideration.
polite.
basic manners.
teen age cave men and women.
parents so caught up in their own
mess, have no time, no desire, no
clue about children.

What I want to say,
you dumb,
ignorant piece of humanity...
how could you possibly think that is
the way to act.
Wouldn't help.
Would it.

I have time to stop and talk with
neighbors without feeling like I have
to hurry and get on to
what ever is next.
I had time to go through the dry
cereal inventory, sorting out the old
stuff and putting the keepers into
attractive plastic containers, and I
even tore off the box top so we
would know what dwelled therein.
Why do we do that?
Find ways to spend more time on
frivolous tasks. Maybe to help us
feel a sense of accomplishment, like
we really are doing something
useful. Something we can actually
complete. I know that's why I like to
work in the yard, now. I used to
hate it, because I was too busy doing
other more important stuff

You know.

FOR YOU.

FOR YOU.

6.

My Time Has Passed

Volunteer
That's what
We do
And we do it well
They need us
They love us
Or not
They want us
To help
We do
Them
Us.

±

Something so mundane
Becoming so important.
Today, I polished my shoes
My black ones, then my brown ones
Buffed my suede ones
New strings in my New Balance all-purpose.
Took my time and did a good job
Didn't feel rushed to get on to something else
Polishing my shoes was the something else
It had been such a long time
Years of dust and dirt
Scuffs and scrapes
Some dents from a few ass kickings
Most times had them done at the shoe store
If at all
Stuff done by others
Busy person living life as it should be lived
Fast
Surface
Forgetting
Value.

I cry over what should be.
I cry over what could be.
I cry over what is.
I also cry over what is.
I sometimes laugh.

±

I'm not dead.
I'm only resting
Waiting
To see which way I go next
New work
New friends
New place
New peace
Retired.
No
Just resting.

±

Still doing
The things I like
Going where
I can
Now
There is more
More time
To do and go and be
More of others
More of me.

Who Served.
A pride cry
For those Who did
The big one
And several
After
Some called to
Some wanted to
Most Came Home
Different
Too many
Did not
Come home
At all
Will we always
War
Will we always
Have to
Glory in winning
With loss
Makes
Way for the
Next one
±
We matter.
Just when I thought I knew it all
I didn't
Just when I thought I was tall
I came up short
Just when I was on top
I fell
Just when I was loved
I lost
Just when I gave up
I got up
We matter.

They've gone under
A good word
For the awfulness
Of a small business owner
Loosing herhis
Investment
Savings
Relationships
Credit
Pride
Security
Dream
So many in our lifetime
Gone under
Pure sadness
I went under
Once
Was enough

±

There's a picture of me
holding my 18 month old son in my arms at
the beach on vacation and we were both in
our bathing suits and
I was comforting this sandy child
who was obviously in some sort of
toddler distress.
The picture is one of many on my screen
saver and every time I see it
I dwell on it for as long as I can
thinking wondering how different things
would be now if
I could only go back to that time
and start again.

When we start reflecting on our lives
what we did and didn't do
what regrets we have and
what we would have done differently
had we had the chance
we can either nose dive into depression and
wallow there until we slowly deteriorate into
nothing
or we can see the past for what it is
when we made choices, decisions
took roads we thought were best
making them on the knowledge and information
we had at the time.
Turns out some of that knowledge
was incomplete
made complete only
in the living of life over a life time
and the information was tainted
by others who were also
traveling on roads that
were decided incorrectly for them.
Either way we have
to deal with the oncoming end.
Some of us want to live it out
no matter what the quality of life,
since we are always teachers and learners
even in death,
and there are reasons for being
here until we're not.
Others of us want only to end
the pain and despair that we feel
and that we most likely
will cause our loved ones
left to take care of us and
our dis-arrayed life.
That's when we think about
how we will cleverly end it all.

When you begin to
spend 10 or 20 percent of your day
thinking about how you could off yourself
so nobody will know that you did
then something is wrong with something.

±±±

We are here to grow
together,
to mutate,
to meld,
to mesh into one human race…
one in love,
in care,
in belief,
in thought,
in word,
in deed and
in spirit.
Then we will be one with the creator…
the universal energy that
has split us all apart like a big bang
to see if and when we will ever
find our way back
to wholeness.

Or we could just be meant to be
A diverse hodge podge of humanity
Trying to figure it out dealing with all the
Crap it brings just being here.

Who knows?

Waiting
For what
Lose weight
Feel better
Better time
Miss my show
Too much
Wrong day
Trouble
Tired
Angry
Sad
Depressed
Too late
Do it
Now
Don't
Wait
Could be
Too
Late.

±

Criticize.

Easy to do
Hard to take

±
When
You
Have
Nothing
To do
And
It
Doesn't
Bother
You
It's
Hard to find
Something
You
Want
To do.

So much to do
So much to still learn
So much noise of knowledge
And pressures to catch up
From outside
Inside
Knowledge
Gone
Wild
Overwhelm and
Exhaustion
Love my
Naps.

±

Gone.
Work, routine, structure, salt, red meat,
chips, ice cream, pimento cheese,
hamburgers, calories, coffee,
alcohol, snacks, cigarettes, etc. etc.
What's left
Life.
Lost what
Found what
What do you think?
Where were you
Where are you now.
Worth it.

Paralyzed in
Memories
Stuck in the past
Nothing but fear
of what's not there
Of what's not known.
What am I going to do today
Nothing.
I've already done that.

±

Took the less traveled path
No one knew what they were doing
Although brave
Took the most traveled path
Not many knew there either.
Keep guessing.
Keep trying.
There might be an answer
±

Will
To avoid
The stuff that could cut my life shorter
Will
To do what I know to do
Can't find it
Where's will.
I've lost will
And it's so dark out here

Three things to take with me
Laid side by side to help remember
Later there
Remembered only two
Need
A better plan.

±

Here's one
Senior senior
Walking down
The sidewalk
Head down
Into phone
Texting
Given
Wide path
Helping hands
Oblivious
High on Hi tech
Senior
Olympian
Working out.

±

Anger.
Deal with it
Can't stuff
It will go
Somewhere else
Inside
Outside
All around
Can't stay
Has to go
Has to be.
How
Where
When
Are
The
Hard parts.

What I owe
What to give back
What
Nothing
Got nothing
Gave nothing
Dissatisfied Depressed
Slow death In place
What's left
Alternative
Self a mess
Wake up call
Opportunities
Not problems
Find value
Find purpose
Now's the time.
What we have left to do
Doesn't really matter.
What we've
Already done
Does.
Unless
There are
Things
We
Can
Do
That
We
Should
Have
Already
Done
And
Can
Do
Now.

Luck.
What's luck got to do with it
Is there any such thing
Luck be a lady
Lucky break
Lucky me
Lucky you
Luck smiled on her
Lucky they got to where they
were going
Before...
Some people got it
Some people don't
Do you think it's so
Does
Luck
Run
Out.

YOUR TURN.

YOUR TURN.

7.

The Road Most Travel

The only way I can make it now day to
day is to believe that all of it
everything that happens
the good and the bad
are part of the larger picture
the grand design
the ultimate truth
the final secret
the revelation of divine purpose
the coming together of it all as one
Otherwise I would have given up long ago
When it all started seeming too real
unfair, inconsiderate, without purpose
with no meaning and downright hateful!
The enormous pain and agony suffered by
most of humanity.
What could possibly be the purpose?
The world is taught about the love a
heavenly father has for his children
and it has become
more and more difficult to see
how that love and our hate, agony,
desperate and mean lives
could possibly coexist even if a
divine all-powerful creator makes it so.
I'm feeling it
thinking it is
not knowing it
but it does help me better understand and
accept and believe
but I don't have to like it.
I don't think I'm supposed to.

Best friends come
And go.
Only the right ones
Stay.
You are one
My best one.
Stay.

±

New Best Friends
Pharmacists
Receptionists
Appointment makers
Cashiers
Bag boys
Technicians
Mechanics
Handy men
Docs
Nurses
Walkers
Hired Help
Meds
All of them
Stay.

One
Two
Three
Docs for me
And then
Four more
Enough
No more
How
Many
Needed
To say
What we know
Well You're just getting old.
Whada I owe you, doc.

±

We don't know it
Until we get here
How life is so short
Now we know to
Be selective
Don't waste time
With what we have
Choose carefully
Don't diddle daddle

When her mother
Was sick
And on her way out
She was there
Day and night and
In between
Little things
Big things
Silly things
Serious things
Clean and dirty things
Holding hands
Sharing tears
And memories
Of mostly good
Loving dedication to
Pay back what she got
She was called
The Angel
When she's ready
Who will her angel be

Maybe me.

Thinking
Of those
Who
Have gone
Before
Missing
Some
Ashamed at
Not missing
Others
Parents
Friends
Work mates
Wives
Husbands
Brothers
Sisters
Aunts and uncles
Some cousins
So many
Waiting for
One of them
To tell me
What's next.

**Old folks
Are slow
To panic**
About dying
We don't worry too much
About that part.
It's the
Going.
The how.
The when.
The how long.
The what's been.
The what's left.

±

Children
Making
Adult decisions
Bring
Adult decisions
For adults to make
For children.
Denying
Blaming
Dividing
Fading
Losing
Regretting
Crying
Dying.

Ailments
Abound
With
Cholesterol
Kidney
Heart
Liver
Stomach
Pancreas
Breast
Teeth stuff
No teeth stuff
Cervix
Knees
Hips
And all the meds lined up in a row
How pretty your gardens grow
Ain't life grand!
±

Friends no more
It's difficult to even see him now
Where did he go
That guy I knew
Disappeared
Into his anger
His regrets
His losses
His sadness
And I can't seem
To bring him
Home.

Getting harder
To remember
To take all those pills
Got a daily dose box
Didn't help
Forgot the box
Wondered
If missing days
Of doses would
Kill me
Nope
I'm still here
At least
For a while.

±

Visiting Questions Unanswered
Do you know me?
Do you want me to stay and visit with
you?
Do you want to watch the game with me?
Our team remember?
Do you want me to go?
Do you want me to raise your head
so you can see better?
Do you want me to go away?
I won't go far
See you next time.

All the time we hear it.
Fixed income
Tight budget
Simplify
Downsize
Next
All that's left
Lays chips and
A walk in closet.
±
She faded
We watched her
Not understanding
Why
She didn't
Get up
Do something
Get out
Enjoy life
We understand
Now.
±
Giving up Giving in
Digging in
Staying put
Don't want to
Don't need to
Why should I
Won't matter
Leave me be
But love me
Still.

What you put in
Is what you get out
Heard that Baloney
Put in years
Get back months
If that
Put in time
Get back less
Put in dollars
Get back pennies
Put in love
Get back loss
What you put in
Is what you put in.
What you get back
Up to you.
±
Place
It keeps changing
There's the
Back Place
The
Future Place
The
Same Place
The
Hoped for Place
And there's
The Now Place.
The Place
We are is
Now.

How we do it
Depends
On where we came from
Who was there
What it was like
What they did
What we did
What we have
      Somebody
      Dollars
      Support
      Community
Who we have
Become.
How we feel about who we are.

        ±
        She settled in to die
        No action
        No friends
        No work, no play
        Endless TV
        Too little sleep
        Easy for us
        Get out
        Do this
        Do that
        Try
        She didn't
        She just didn't
        Guess what
        I know.

Home.
It's where the start is
Place of love and care
For growing and knowing
Finding
Becoming
Leaving
Visiting
Less and less
Making
Another home
Filling it
Learning
Growing
Searching
Leaving
Looking for heart
Found some
Lost some
Lost heart
Lost self
Back
At the Start
Looking for
Home.
It's where the heart is.
Heart
It's where the home is.

Don't take it.
> Let 'em have it!
> Don't let 'em have it!
> Stand your ground
> There's a lot to lose
> Freedom
> Pride
> Checkbook
> Keys
> Home
> Self
> Life.
> Hold on to what you got
> Till you don't.
>> ±

Dependent.
Used to be
My children
At tax time
Now
It's me
On them
At
Their
Time
±

Love life
Sure
It's the only one we've got
Sure
This time
Not sure
Maybe more.

Last night
Like many other nights
Of late
In deep dark
Sleeplessness
Replays of
Days and
Years
Toss and tumble me
Inside
With frowns mostly
Some smiles
Regrets and
Successes
A few
Mostly gone.
And now
Up ahead
Seeing those who
Are there
Already
What's going on
The lives they live
Their eyes
Tell so much
And make me
Wonder
Can I do it.

Don't care for me dearest Tina
I know
That I can do it
Don't wait on me dearest Tina
I am still able
To set the table
Boil
Cut
Peel
Cook and sew
Get up and go
So don't cry for me dearest Tina
I know you aughter
Cause you're my daughter
But it's too soon now
I'm just not ready
Don't do this to you.

±

Fear is a scary thing
What's next Who's next
What corner do we turn to find what's best.
Who to trust
Doctors
Lawyers
Politicians
Relatives
Brokers
Companies
Hospitals
Don't let them get you down.
We're still here
Alive still
Smart still
We know.   Most of the time.

How to keep going
To not give up
Find the
Spark
Hope
Strength
Courage
Desire.
We have known
Hard times
Young ones
Don't know
Don't want to hear it
Oh what marvels we could share
Oh what input to avoid
Pot holes
Walls
Ditches
Fires
Losses
Grief
Lots of grief.
How do we do it
In spite of.
That's just
Us.

Clichés

It's never too late
Get a new lease on life
Everything's gonna be alright
You're only as young as you feel
Get up, get going
Don't worry about it
Help is just around the corner
Blue skies are up ahead
It's not the years in your life
but the life in your years
Live every day like it's your last
It ain't over till it's over.
Helpful
Not a bit.
Sometimes it IS over
Before it's over.

That part.

Let's say
Tomorrow is the last day
For everybody
What
Would you do
Today
What would you want
Today to be
A soft rain
Falling quietly
From slightly
Cooled grey
Skies
Scotch on the
Side table
Light
Classical
Piano on
Time Warner Music
Candles lighting us
Both in
Cozies
Lying
In bed
Waiting
Holding
Remembering
Thankful.

Closets
Attics
Basements
Storage
All that stuff
Gathered
Go through it
Clean it out
Like the clutter
In life
Who's interested
Who cares
Not the kids
Why put them through it
There are some things
That are hard to trash
Ok with replacement
Some
New stuff
But don't throw out the old
It is us.

That's It.

Or is it?

in or out
feels good
to sit
to rock
to hum
to go numb
to forget
to wallow
careful
balance
comfort
rock
but
don't rock away.

YOUR TURN. WRITE IT DOWN.

FOR YOU. YOUR THOUGHTS.

! p.20 Family
p.25 This Stirred famous ____ remember
                                        this!

? p.33 This is not good ____
                              Beautiful!
p.34

p.35 frankly ____ Sweet!

p.36 when I ____ other ____ -sweet)
        beautiful, unconditional love.
p.40 so Told custody ____ poignant
p.46 the other ____ -nasty -not
        exactly ____, but....

p.47 -both poems ____ ////////// ↗
+51-54 l.# 51
pp.48-49,50 +51 challenges of aging body-
        illness, infirmity
p.50 There is no better ____ - ///// -
                    141
        especially of a child

YOUR NOTES.

p. 52 Reinventing ourselves — counter out
of that of "I like me as I am."

p. 55 Hill + stair gets thin — funny

p. 57 Fun while insanely jiggling

p. 60 - Rejining sweet daily schedule

p. 70 Drille by Arles does the work +
build protest a block?

p. 71 self help — funny. Any —
need is $

p. 72-76 The Cloud by puts sethopeca
a life + depression. not the axis
to live is Okay.

p. 77 good March! flight of hope

p. 78 love the lost put it slightly so
long i are the dust feels at home

p. 82 She not so good at slight things i we
one of several poems they
understand by slightly or saying he
didn't before

p. 83 By needle Busy life is it too late
to make y contribution?

142

p. 85 several poems - old people can
still help solve the (world) problem

Jim R. Rogers. That's me. A 77 year old grandfather of four boys and the father of two men and a woman. My marriage to Sally Z. Hare has changed my life, giving new meaning and new directions to my search for questions and answers.

After graduating from UNC Chapel Hill and 3 years in the Army, I worked in television, advertising and as a commercial director in Charlotte, Atlanta, New York City, and in Los Angeles before changing careers and becoming a Parenting and Family Life Educator, working in inner city Los Angeles and then back in the Southeast and Coastal Carolina University.

Now with the company that Sally and I own and operate, still learning, inc., I am still working with parents and families as they try to find the way toward the most effective parenting they can offer their children. I was a columnist for a regional specialty newspaper for 15 years and will soon publish a collection of my parenting and family essays from those years.

This first offering of very free verse poems and scattered narrative, Starts And Stops Along The Way, is in part a personal memoir, observations, opinions and philosophies, hopes and dreams, successes and failures of a life lived so far and in sharing I invite others on the same journey to continue working toward making your lives a joy to live and to remember to stay connected with your best traveling partner, yourself.

Thank you for reading and writing with me.

Jim

jimrogers@sc.rr.com

p. 86 Dogs — best. We we raise
the journey is early, we get out
& slow down.

p. 88 All of life — thoughts he was,
to — do really proud, and
thats not the place of the
late — Rte now.

p. 110 The only way — there must be
some kind of definite plan.
p. 115 when her mother was upset — "she
will be removed. Maybe not it

p. 148 what you put in
"what you get out is p N yc"

145

CPSIA information can be obtained at www.ICGtesting.com
Printed in the USA
LVOW040239140512

281573LV00004B/18/P